ONGOING PORTRAITS

BY Walter Pavlich   1985

Barnwood Press

DATE DUE

Arts-In- Corrections
Ext. 3454

ONGOING PORTRAITS

Walter Pavlich

First printing
ISBN 0-935306-33-1

Some of the poems in this book have appeared in *Another Chicago Magazine*, *The Atavist*, *Bloomsbury Review*, *Cincinnati Poetry Review*, *CutBank*, *Concerning Poetry*, *Fedora*, *Fusion West*, *Greensboro Review*, *Hawaii Review*, *Hubbub*, *Mississippi Mud*, *Northern Lit Quarterly*, *Northwest Magazine*, *Oregon Arts News Bulletin*, *Oxford Magazine*, *Poetry Now*, *Portland Review*, *Purchase Poetry Review*, *The Silverfish Review*, *Swallow's Tale*, *Tar River Poetry*, *Visions*, *Willamette Week*, *Night House Anthology*, *Pudding* anthology of separation and divorce, and the *Anthology of Magazine Verse and Yearbook of American Poetry*, 1981, 1985.

"Notes Toward an Ongoing Portrait" is based on a line of David Schubert's.

Thanks to Ray Gonzalez, editor of the Mesilla Poetry Series in which "Climbing Down Stars," "Elegy," "A Recommendation for the Dead," and "Loadstones" first appeared as the pamphlet, *Loadstones*.

Thanks also to the Ragdale Foundation for a scholarship and the time to work on several of these poems, and to the Oregon Arts Commission for a fellowship to help me continue with my work.

Many of these poems would not have been possible without the encouragement and support of John Haislip, Fred Chappell, James Welch, Richard Ford, Sandra McPherson, and Richard Hugo.

Publication of this book was assisted by a grant from the Indiana Arts Commission.

The cover photo shows The Herculean Trio of the author's father, George Pavlich (standing), Al Holland (handstand), and Sam Loprinzi.

Graphics by Barbara LaRue King.

The Barnwood Press
Rt 2   Box 11C
Daleville, IN 47334

Printed in The United States of America.

For George, Eleanor, Paul, Melinda, and Ruby

Contents

People think Bud is crazy or lost or silent but really he is in a state of grace.

Francois Paudras on Bud Powell

After Seven Years, I Remember
the Blind Mathematician

for Paul Hansen

After school I watched you
muttering numbers to yourself in the empty classroom,
then on the blackboard you traced
a formula, paused, and erased it.
I ran home to the piano, felt each note
linger and die beautiful beneath my hands.
I haven't learned much since then.
You knew we cheated on every test.

How did geometry rise out of that haze
the eyes scraped pure, blue, and bottomless?
There are at least two kinds of darkness
and one of them dissolves
the blooming rhododendron,
another tugs the string that keeps me awake
and walking into tomorrow.

The Shadow of the Child

Because I had not been at ease for months
often lying face down into motel sheets
twisting and rolling in madness of 4:30 a.m.
Because a man on graveyard shift
turns away from the boiler and thinks
of his child at home with its shallow cough.
Because the dead follow me everywhere
even into the faces of a lover.

Was this why leaves welcomed me back
to their world, clinging wet to my neighbor's roof?
The streetlamp became the light I had watched
for snow by. So I gathered the shadow
of the child I used to be in my arms
and leaning against the cold window
we realized those leaves had been abandoned
in their brittle hours.

It was then we made a promise to each other
that no one else could hear.

The Bridgetender

I wake up to the face
of a fifty-year-old man.
He had lost his job as bridgetender
been asleep among the gears
when the freighter hit.

We have coffee and talk rivers.
Mine was thick. We'd catch
suckers and smash their heads
with a brick. And in the middle
an island of beasts we never swam to.

Each slow day grows slower.
He knows that. He knows
his mouth is a broken music box.
I repeat our names to the mirror.
They come back empty sacks.

He's deaf in his left ear
says mornings grind him down to rubble.
He sets a bottle on the table
"This is another river."
I drink and tell him to go to hell.

If I were his son or brother
I'd take his weak hand in mine
and tell him one good story—
a lie. He says he's going to work.
I tell him "Watch out for ships."

He opens the door
"You can't even feel them when they hit."

Revisiting the Field

We learned how to lose every Friday night:
Jefferson, Madison, every damned team in the league.
I can still hear those cleats
echoing off the school walls.
Remember the last game,
when Henry ran that punt back in the mud?
Didn't we all block big as trees?
Later, the crowd outside, drunk, too cheap
to buy tickets, threw insults
until Wallace herded them to their cars.
It was ourselves we hated:
the coach, the cheap shots in practice.
Knocking our friends down,
out of breath, out of confusion.
Isn't it all bull-in-the-ring now?
The floodlights, blurring crowd?
The terrible smack of our hearts
against our lives.

Drinking in the Boneyard

All our stammering gets us nowhere.
From nowhere to here: a hillside
of veiled bones
a graveyard like any other.
Should we baptize the marble
sprinkle bourbon on every stone?
Maybe a few drops would open
one mouth and words would rise
in whorls of old music.
Have you ever heard a dead man sing?
It leaves a tiny burning in the skull.

You might find yourself on your knees
bothered by generations
you've never met, whose breath
you never tasted. You might lie
on your back, give thanks
that you can't grab hold of the moon
and stick it in your backpocket.
You'd probably hear someone say
"dum vivimus vivamus" touch
your lips and find them moving
almost bursting with names.

The next morning you watch
a bird outside the window
singing from a leafless tree.
You tap the glass with your fingernail
murmur "crow, birch"
and his heart matches the beat
of his wings. You wish
the bird was watching you
even as he flies away.
You remember the girl who placed

a pillow in the oven, who reached for the gas.

You realize the wilderness you've built
over the years with eyes and hands
and sit by the window until evening.
You imagine the men with shovels
cutting into earth. You know
their steel dulls with every blow
as darkness gently hugs the roof.

Millionaire

for Bruce Latimer

Because we had been through it
whatever it takes
for two to empty an evening
until the hours drop off
like the iced leaves of your favorite tree.
We walked. Walked the downtown
streets filling and repeating with snow
saying things like "If I were in Nice
I know it would be different" or
"Imagine enough green and that woman."

Both of us womanless
not mentioning the wind
we found a station wagon nosed in a snowbank
white exhaust pluming.

We did not know
if he was drunk or dead
or believing at last in the implosion
of his wife's heart.

His window disappearing
he said "Fellas, I dreamed
I was a millionaire"
and backed slowly out of our eyes.
He
his own ghost
and unafraid.

A steel wind scattered our footprints
uncountable powder stars.
He was not the sadness
we thought we needed.
Not the one who would let us know.

Remembering St. Regis

for Wayne Challeen, on the St. Regis Fire Crew

Challeen, I can't get the moon off my back,
smoke out of my nose.

Can you feel it mornings, premature wheeze
over coffee, brown lungs stuttering?

St. Regis sticks us forever, something calcified
inside too sharp for pillows. Forever lunar

flame until fingers curl a last grasp.
We bought enough beers to choke gutters.

One night, remember the plan:
saw down every roadsign, every indication

to strangers the place ever breathed.
More than once, four drinks above the day,

they called us to some mountain-saddle on fire,
all dark long digging toward the sun.

But Challeen, I'll tell you this,
whatever hell we knew is smoke

climbing a stack in Kansas.
Maybe further.

And given the chance we'd do it again—
dance those songs starglare lent us

high above our theater of heat, even though
I've forgotten the names of those men

I thought we were, the words we toasted
chased by lies and the black walk home alone.

A long time it finally takes to say
I quit, my knees are broken fenceposts,

my eyes the home of scorched animals.
Numb, with one last paycheck each,

we climbed the bus, treeshadows flickering windows,
a beercan rolling up and back

and not enough gears for where we wanted to go.

For My Father

Then he did not know joy.
Day after day at ugly 5:15
he'd park the dustblack Plymouth
climb out and walk downstairs
to the basin. Lava soap, dirty brush,
could not wash thirty years of shop away.
I thought his heart too was metal.
When we drove down to Front
he pointed "there" where his father
had sold meat. "They broke down
his building in two days."
And he wept for the first time
into his thick hands.
Later at the green square house
where his father had died alone
in a kitchen chair he talked
of the last slav and the bill collectors
knocking at the back door during supper.
Bohunk one after another
lost seven thousand miles of hope
to this port town.
I don't give a damn what they say
some men live to die and become saints.
And though my father cannot hear me now—
his ears lost to machines that wore them down,
I can say horseshit to the Ironworkers
when the check arrives. I, the angry son
shouting into the barren, iron ears.

Minuet in G 1941

He lumbers up the stairway
under a ninety-pound sack of flour.
He'll wrestle the circus strongman
tomorrow night and win
thirty-five dollars.
Later he'll look in the mirror
at the bruise darkening on his chin
the quarter-size welt on his temple
and lie in bed all night
counting the stairs
the green in his pocket
hoping it'll all be different tomorrow.

Five six it never changes
nine ten step after step
until none of the sacks remain.

She carries three plates
up each arm
fixes her hair
like Jeanette MacDonald.
She makes thirteen dollars a week
and wants to buy a piano.
She doesn't know she's pretty.

Maybe they meet at an Oddfellow's dance
on a slow August night.
Maybe the band won't stop playing
and they dance to the moon and back.

He can't buy her any piano.
She tries to smile.
She tries to brush
the flour out of his shirt.

Staring out over her shoulder
what does he see, some grace
his thick back won't touch?
Why do his arms loosen around her
light and useless?

Grandfather Crow and the Grave

Here on Mount Calvary
you tilt over a city.
Ten years ago you died,
today your hand let go my shoulder,
white hair stopped burning my cheek.
I'm sorry they gave me your name,
even water will rest in pools.
When did the trade-off begin:
bone for black feather, blood for air,
long flights over the town
you won't ever leave.

You fly nights over my tracks,
counting kneemarks in snow.
Almost home now, I'll go inside
to the gathering loss, draw curtains,
and ignore your hands pressed against the window.
Stunned, frightened, my life is stalling.
Nothing will live in this house except you.

Someone breathing remains. Though no
brother, he waits for us
in the corner, mute in a chair.
Fresh walls fail the old light.
He's weeping and his days
mutter into his nights. We drink
his last bourbon and tell him
"Gosho, you live and need nothing."
We leave thieves of his weak horizon.

Last Call to Uncle Willie

Willie, I am tired of
chewing on your bittersweet liver,
two thousand miles from
your child-sized coffin
poured deeply into the ground.
Maybe one of the rivers
in heaven or hell
flows one hundred proof.
You kept reaching for absolution
with ice cubes and sparkling lava,
burning your legs to stubs
the size of my fists,
which are trying to love you
this one last time.
There was no way
to amputate the fear
you tried to die with.
Working with vodka and wood
you made pornographic lamps,
forties-style breasts
that plump my basement
with sexless light.
No one was able to swirl your
limbs from desire and prayer.

Your wife sold your wheelchair
cheap to a couple expecting
the worst. She wanted to
give it to the lawn
in the always rain
for the next pick-up
of the thrown away.

I don't know what makes
a man want to be more

liquid danger than he already is.
Sometimes you'd call me up
so drunk even the telephone lines
could not straighten your voice.
I've forgotten most of what
you used to try and tell me
during your blurry monologues
but am relieved and ashamed to say
you'll never find my new number.

Father and Son

In the unlit kitchen
we laughed and drank an afternoon to hell.
Words and bottle gone
we sat quiet for an hour.
I said "Father, I haven't learned a goddamned thing."
He said nothing, knowing I'd barely learned
how to screw a girl or spit
in the world's eye if it needed it.
I slept head in arms on the table
and tried to love every mistake
he'd ever made.

What Bourbon Sends

He came here early century
to avoid war, cut meat and drink nights
alone in the kitchen. I'm second generation
the first traitor. The dead can't see.
That was a lie some priest told to keep us
from learning our groins. My father hated the war
but likes those movies. He says I worship tin gods
and pours another drink. I say drink until we can't
lose our names. Sometimes bourbon brings you
face to face with the dead. My name rhymes
with sonofabitch and all my anger is old.
I need those hands, that dark wine and words
like bocko and bakala. I'm still here.
My father's still deaf. His best friend is bohunk
and they drink everyday but Sunday.
Was there something in Grandpa's last breath?
Some curse to remember? I know better.
I'm a sip off the old drunk. He's buried
with the dagoes and that's my name in the marble.

Explanations to the Mirror

Two hours along a quiet road
you tramp the first tracks
in woods heavy with snow.
Those pines always bend
to the darkness of snow.
Grandmother, is this how it was?
The corners folding, the room
crashing down in white?

You wake next morning
world dead in your arms
and know the damned stay damned.
Everything dark survives:

the eye is a pin is a river
is a madman in the corner laughing with the walls.
Where did the angel go?
Who put water in his tears?
Mother crow swallows the air
that drunk men burn in their sleep.

No. Tell the mirror you need old hands.
Why old women dance in the ceiling of your bones.
That light never knocked. It entered.
And she dumb from light left you
with one tree leaning in its nightmare.

Maybe your dreams are wrong.
Maybe you dissolve like weather leaving another heap
for sky to wind down on.
Ashes, ashes we all break down.

Old Stories, New Lies

I have lived with quiet men
all my life. I have told many lies.
Maybe not enough. My grandfather
did not die alone in a kitchen chair.
He left on the fourth floor
waiting for a blue crack
in the walls, flying through a hole
in plaster. His wife's arteries
stiffened. Blood traveled a slow route
to her brain. Next door a blind girl
counted her steps to the store. She had
six mean brothers. Dagoes, Grandpa said.
During the Depression he gave them
meat cheap. When his shop went belly-up
they would not answer their door.

Near the end he drank Cribari
evenings at six-thirty
watched the fights on Fridays.
I tried his hat on once. It fit
like a bowl on a stick.
Fourteen years later I went back
to the house. A few of his
empty jugs were still in the basement.
The woman said I could have them.
She'd found a picture upstairs
behind the bed, kept it for years.
Every morning I wake up with his name.
I didn't tell her it wasn't him.

Ruth, Mt. Tabor Nursing Home, 1972

The nurses can ignore
a bed but not the pink-faced
cries of a woman whose screams
rasp each afternoon down
to the bone.
Only her hair calm
and sleeping white.

I am just a boy who mops
the iced-tea spilled, and urine
threading towards the door.

Sometimes I hear my father
muttering little dust-sounds
to himself in the basement,
among the wrenches his hands
have warmed, among the boxed histories
of his blood, and a mattress
that helped make my stillborn brother.

I am afraid
when the dying
won't use words.

Damage Report

You must have heard the news by now.
He's gone. Dead at eighty-eight.
I can picture the gravestone:
"1892 to a funeral of zinfandel slavs".
Every bohunk in southeast Portland there.
Black suits, black wine, and more wine.
Willie couldn't make it. He drank one leg away,
stays in bed knowing he's next.
Remember the last time at Petrich's house?
Wasn't it you, me, Simich and the old man
drinking away six feet of heavy dirt?
He couldn't find his village on the map
somewhere in the green hills behind Spljet
some land between Dalmatia and the sea.
You're right Paul—we face the days ahead
with a broken gyroscope. Look behind us though
to the old croat treated worse than a thin horse.
Jammed through Ellis Island, half his name
thrown in a wastebasket.
How about thirty years in the same metalshop
working for some sonofabitch named Hanna.
Until one Monday morning he calls you
into his office and says "Go home. You're too old."

I dream of going back and beating up
that kid who used our name for a joke.
I'd scrape his face on the dirt road
and never say a word. Other bad news:
due to east wind and an ice storm,
our walnut tree uprooted. They sawed it up
that same day for fifty dollars. So much for memory.
If you write back, send your letter care of Lutz's Bar.
All revenge is soft there flowing back from the mirror.

Elegy

for Helen Johnson

Now you're back, my dear sister, after thirty years.
I'll tell you what I know:
all things are lightly won and darkly paid.

From your second-story window, you watched
a bird shudder, then dip into the stone bath,
and knew a breath could live on its own.
In your insomnia, our father
spoke of a gentle passing. It shook you
all the more—too many nights of wings
feathering the attic. You murmured for days,
and once "The roses are afraid, someone hold their hands."
We looked out to the ragged stems,
our lives pared down to ugly marrow.
Now you're back telling me there's no difference
between window and mirror, birds rove the blue
because there never is a home. I've been listening
to my birds. They say begin again, wishing
isn't enough anymore. They're right.
I'm learning to live without comfort.

The Carousel of Birds

for Verlena

I wander your apartment
afraid my words are children at school
who say the wrong things about home.
Remember that afternoon
when starlings like bell-tongues
seemed to swing back, then rang
your south window alive?
A carousel of birds, their feather-compass
set on glass. Months later, still cemented with blood,
three feathers pale, the color of dead lightbulbs.

If I touch your books,
eight open packs of cigarettes,
Tammy Wynette record,
a manuscript safe in plastic
in the refrigerator's desert dark,
will you know it?
Do objects know the fingerheat of strangers?

Like an August evening in your mind
the cumulus of mania built up
something cloudy, glazed and wrong—
wet gravel shimmering, books nodding off the shelf,
a dinner for none set for two.

You hid it all in rouge,
bright chenille,
baths a full morning long,
while you made the list of betrayals.

Your husband offering an insult:
zinnias from your garden
leaning lost in summer dusk.

When he walked away, past attendants

into the harsh language of waxed floors,
did you shut him like a closet door?

Your mirror hurt.
I know how a face almost
like your own can ache.
Four eyes from the same face,
threads of filament cut,
all staring solo.

But you have returned from the blur,
those sad years peel
like veneer too long in the heat.
I'll need you here
if wind trills the screens,
if the birds come careening back.
You see, I want the window broken,
these rooms deep and heavy with birds.

Wondering Over the Poet Thomas James
(1946-1974)

All I have are rumors
of your leaving and the few dozen

poems you finally became.
Was it the Berryman one-and-a-half

a slow-motion somersault
to powder and ice?

Or reamed-out hotel room
a revolver tepid on the rug?

Twenty-eight when you disappeared
into the tender nothing you imagined.

I have already outlived you
though I to and fro

in the gray insomniac's cage
sometimes lick a poisoned dream.

I'm not asking for reasons
guess that you splintered

from one into one thousand needs.
Maybe found yourself dissolving

like a puddle in a burning afternoon
until all you had was one choice

and made it—marry the air.
I'd like to think you're still

disturbing our living
still serving your delicate warrants

on this world. Today I believe
we have little in common

except affection for the insatiable urge
not sad thirst. Wherever you decided

to live I see you in a garden
kneeling over Chinese lanterns

trying to heal
their orange and quiet wounds.

Piano Serenade for Eleanor

The mailman will not stop
his coughing to listen.
A pedal-moan begins the afternoon
its echo an andante of memories
softened by rain.

Poor:

a book read
over and over wishing
for a somehow different end

a Depression-quiet father
drunk in the attic creaking
above his family's dreams
curses bursting the night-blue heat

a sister tired
of fainting in public
of not knowing what's wrong
eyelids fluttering under
a chain of strangers.

Long hunger created a need
for the frivolous. For you—a piano
and a teacher who called you
"my charming student"
who watched you breathe in
your first symphony.

No one knows what made him
put the sour barrel in his mouth.
Things were picking up . . .

It is still possible to love
a piano, this patient thing

outside your body.
But tell me, how many
never-hads and have-nots
balance in your floured hands?
And could his explosion, then deafness
be called a kind of song?

On Not Growing Up With Fireflies

Fireflies ascend the rain-coming air,
each arc governed by the need
for another light like its own.
They give up feeding
and just swallow air
or the flight-scent of a luminous mate.
I missed them as a boy
too many clouds spilling
over to douse them.

But even then I knew
my eyes would not save me
for what I wanted to see.
I used a cracker-hole
to pierce the world—
crows hooked on a telephone pole,
water lifting out of the sea.

I can view them now
in the amphitheatre of the Midwest
bits of dry lightning
cruising and resting.
Bewildered moths veer toward
their intermittent illumination.
I have faith in these aviators
on fire with their on-again
off-again nocturnal ignition,
these quick sparks of eternity.

Climbing Down Stars

My Father, Seventy, At the Campanile, Pisa

Spiralling up this interior route,
he nudges past breathworn tourists
to the top. Following patient steps
of three nuns, I imagine spidery veins
latticing blue on the white maps of their legs.
When I see him again, he's leaning
no hands over the brass rail,
figurehead of this tilting Italian afternoon.

I want to tell him, move back—
that the eyes of marble dissolve,
fathoms of air over greenfired grass
will only support him in the photograph
snapped by the retired fireman afraid of ladders.

By now he's a stranger, his arms
along the dried shoulders of two nuns,
the other with camera, positioning them
in shy French.

Winding down bone stairs
I've lost my father somewhere
years above me throwing smiles
like pennies into a glass sea.

Father, if you tire of high breeze
glazing your face, come back.
It is dark. We don't climb down
stars to die, our hands far from home,
this tower everfalling.

Old Woman Dreaming of Venice

I am a glass horse beginning in fire,
an old woman afraid of the baths,
the ugly crank of faucets turning.
Light scratches my eyes awake
and I know they are coming,
two or three of them and the boy,
his hands chilled and smooth as wax.
I let him drown my breasts,
wander my front heavy as floursacks,
his dark heat tightening the air.

I eat nasturtiums,
show him Venice postcards,
my accordian dreams—
the Bridge of Sighs,
the glassblower's horse
cooling in the straw.
I tell him there is dirty water
in my veins, inside my head
fish nudge and roll but won't eat.
I'm not sinking like Venice.
When I sing, I taste liquid glass.

The Room

You know something's wrong, but won't admit it—
behind the closet door, another door.
You climb the stairs, find a room
where there never was a room. Windows
to north, south and west.
A gray perpetual weather.
You sit at the desk waiting for dark.
It never comes. Once a month
a man who looks like your grandfather
shows up and asks for food.
You tell him you haven't eaten in years.
Bones in his face show through
like sticks. He stands there crying
"Get out. This is my home."

One day you think there's a bird
outside you can help. You pound the glass
with your fists. He hovers near the window
then drops in the yellow grass.
You try to remember a name, the date
of your birth. No luck.
Even the hands running over your face
seem foreign. You decide enough is enough
and reach for the stairs. They ascend
in a brass spiral. You feel more tired
than ever before and sit on a step,
head between your knees.
You will live in this room forever.

Two Ghazals for Zarzyski

We were born to quiet men,
cast-iron fathers brooding

hard over nickels at the bar.
They talked to their machines

before the morning switched on.
Remember the way a man

can breathe into his hands
and taste what's wrong.

We still have a chance
or a change

or something like gentle
is another word for ok.

Remember a way we can
feel better than ourselves.

———————————

Drown her if you have to.
Skip her like a stone downstream.

Tie your nightmares to a branch
touching water, let them

beg and call with the tides.
Bathe in the river

of what you don't know,
in moss-light, in mosquitos

busy with dusk.
Assemble yourself again by the stars.

Loadstones

for John Haislip

You try to forget the words:
bookish, shy, a coward.
Your slough of years ago has stiffened,
frozen in a deep wind. That wind hung
crow on a treelimb, left him burning
and he dropped heavy in the snow.
No one gathered him up, dogs looked away.
Your loadstone is now the black shawl
found by children in the river. They use it
for a dark game until one runs home
through the brush crying mother.
For awhile you believed all this was nonsense.
Now you pray for anything, even a nightmare
to break the crumbling circle. Try to remember
something simple, a dirt road, dandelions
breathing the air. Quit memorizing the dead,
their collection of stories and bones.
Where is the cry of joy that first
roused you into song? You're just a bearwatcher
looking for stars in his blue heart.
He's staring down through the night,
never at you. Never at the footprints
walking home, left behind.

As We Dark Awaken

Once you lose, the waterway's open.
She says Walter, lie down
to the blue turn of sky,
leafmeal long buried in snow.
This day of fifty-six cigarettes

we use windows and lamplight
to watch a river nudge the bank away.
Know the hills are not soft.
From here, two clocks run finally down.
We break days in two, afternoon

by sleep. And when we awaken dark,
we've forgotten the bird-thrust and fall
and believe his black heart
will have any alley, oak or air.
Now it's breathing, the rising water.

Ruined fields hold the only light.
When I prayed, it was to answer by dawn.
But anything that ancient has lost
its motherface to the red-eyed men.
What's caught tangles in the others.

She says no, and repeats blue blue for the wait.
For if crow returns, no wall will save us.
Better to forget the names we're given.
In his circling, it's too late now.
Two stories up, helpless in evening and water.

Elegy for James Wright

I spent the first nine years of my life
thinking the Oregon Artificial Limb Co.
repaired broken trees.
I thought the men were doctors
lathing wooden arms for cedars.
But the doctors did not come
when that October storm
laid my trees out lengthwise.
I walked each one from thick roots
to their tangle of branches.
On Camelhump Hill I found a nest
and scraped mud from the windbeaten home.
For three weeks the birds did not come back.

An epileptic drank coffee in the cafe
to keep himself from sleeping all day dead.
Customers would not eat
during his blue electric fits.
When his head banged the table
cigarette butts jumped from the ashtray
and coffee spilled over his fingers
from the cup frozen to his hand.
You'd hear him stamping the tile
all the way into the kitchen.
The cook turned up the radio.
We said "It's ok, he'll be back soon."

Dying is getting too popular.
It would be nice to think
that he died happy
reaching for a bough in some small meadow.
Maybe as the ribcage settled
his air seeped out little by little
and redwings gathered up his body
lifted him skyward to a horse

waiting among the clouds.
Did all of Ohio go with him?
That day a man told me
"I'm sad, tired and running out of fire."
Me too, brother. I'm sick of the lessons
I'm learning. Only the epileptic
can call him now. At least
one good man has found his home.

A Recommendation for the Dead

for Richard Hugo

He could gut our hearts,
leave us pulsing on any shore.
Some died there. Some found enough light
in midnight water and found home.
Tell the mailman this is a letter
of recommendation for the dead.
Tell him he left no forwarding address.
Who you want hobbled past humming
"When you're smiling, when you're smiling"
and didn't turn around.

Does this window weigh the world
and isn't it heavier: November, fingernails,
sky, the bed that always said yes?
Snow needs a partner, needs me more
than ever. But I move in a dream—
rain through a broken ceiling,
rain smearing portraits on the floor,
faces rankled.

Who you want is gone. Can't you see
I limp and fall, twist and rise?
Go away. Bourbon's the wheel,
stars are the road. Kiss my forehead,
is it grim?

Right now, I'm more alive
than I care to be.
I can live with that.

After Midnight Work

The fan works its neck
sore in the black air.
He'd give most anything
for a dirt-cool dream
basement-deep.
He knows how sleep softens
the corners of a body
how lack of it glazes
like a vague layer of jam.
Even certain stars
no matter where they crash
are too much traffic
in his skull.

Ten million volts of lightning
jerk down from heaven
shattering the horizon.
Pin-thin lodgepole pines
divide into ghosts.
It will be enough fire
to melt several days
and nights together.

Each swing of his pulaski
will puncture the earth
in order to save it.
What it won't save
is the marriage
he disinters every night
that digging up
of what should have been.

He remembers how their house
smelled after her final leaving
like a cigarette almost out
like boiling dirt.
That surprise worse than a hand
realizing a glove full of sparks.

The Diver

A breeze forty years old
blew up a memory in this couple,
his willow leg dragging like an anchor
he cannot carry. The ferris wheel
frozen in its rusted circle,
most of the danceband dead,
the tar walkways gray
dreaming pennies and broken heels.

She nods to the pool
that trembles with rainwater and cans,
where he dove eight times (she says nine)
for the locket that slipped from her neck.

Each time he rose he smiled
while a man soggy with beer
flushed over her thighs.

When he felt it shine in his palm
he gave it back to her and they laughed
at the faces stretched like years.

These were the faces they now own.
I believe in them
as I may never believe again.

So I faithless sleeper tell you this
as you turn in sleep murmuring words
soft as moonwater in a glass,
that a man with one leg
or one eye or one heart
still dives, if not through water
then through leafrains, wet wind.
Through a season so clear with love and danger
even birds will witness my hands
closing again over nothing and you.

I'd Like to Invent

an evening where you and I
could wander rhododendrons free
in the dusk of a water skipper
day. If your face would not
abandon itself to a heron,
the blue climb of a teal,
I would better know
which one of you to hold,
which to disenchant.

We try to ignore the ordinary
by stepping out of a winter afternoon
into the basement mausoleum.
The dead are always surprised
to find themselves disengaged
and floating blind
like albino bottomfish.
Love, they know betrayal—
it begins and ends with breathing.
We'd like to believe they can't
hear us. We kiss to loosen the air.

Notes Toward an Ongoing Portrait

We will never argue over headless lamps
or davenports oiled smooth
by the love-patterns of others.
We won't scrape the months away
from check to check, or blame
the baby's quirks on bickering
overheard from the swampy womb.

No, never the opportunity
to dilute each other's faces
wandering monotony and rain
over the years' mornings.

Did we really vary
the mood of the grass, broken,
where we layered our skin
with maple shade?

When we've become somebody else,
I'll lean back and say
they loved each other and the ghost
and the ghost was never boring.

I always want to believe
your hands are a welcome,
our whorls not quite aligned,
your tongue a rose-moth
fluttering against my outlaw teeth.

My instinct for you
is a pure bell.

What do I do though,
when I catch on the edges
of your long-distant voice,
translate your face by memory?

The Lullaby of Spontaneous Combustion

Before the moon closed our eyes,
we would begin to drowse
during the stories, those talky lullabies
of shade and water, of a porch
with white iron chairs,
nude backs and a breeze.
Then there's the one about a woman
in Florida whose body made
its own flames just once.
How all they found was a foot
in a black satin slipper,
a backbone, and her skull reduced
to the size of an orange.
If she woke, her belly already on fire,
which sounds did she try,
the bedsprings releasing,
before her voice found its way
to her combustible mouth.

Sunday Aquarium

Sunday morning and the fish alone.
Some dozing, some disturbed
by bubbles like furious mercury rising.
They cannot forget
the angles of their confinement,
nosing their borders and retreating.
But we have smuggled our way
to yet another place a husband
cannot find us.

Blind arm over blind arm
we are the starfish,
a boneless groping in slow water,
curious for the next tide
to light our senses.
Or are we the leaf fish
whose glassy invisible fins
suspend it in a perpetual fall?

We'll never mean anything
to them. These floaters look
more serious than they need to be.
We are creatures bound
to walk away and remember.
Certain starfish tear or lose
an arm, a pastel wanderer,
and begin a new one.
Others cannot and learn
to hold tighter and feel with less.

Born in 1955 in Portland, Oregon, Walter Pavlich has lived most of his life in that state and in Montana, where he received his MFA, worked as a firefighter in the woods, and ranged widely as visiting writer. Recently the quality of his poetry has received recognition in the form of a scholarship from The Ragdale Foundation, a fellowship from The Oregon Arts Commission, and first prizes in the Willamette Week Poetry Contest for 1984 and 1985. Poems in *Ongoing Portraits* have been published in magazines throughout the United States. His pamphlet, *Loadstones*, is available from Mesilla Press.